To my
dearest
friend
Kathie

When life hurts,
God shows us He cares
through one another.
I am here for you.
I care.

INSPIRATION FOR YOU

BE *E*NCOURAGED

ELLYN SANNA

A DAYMAKER GREETING BOOK

I am thinking of you today,

saying a prayer

that you might take heart,

gather strength,

and be inspired

to face your life

with new energy.

May you be encouraged...

When You Are Afraid

When You Are Overwhelmed

When You Are Sorrowing

When Life Seems Hopeless

I have...

learned that when a baffling

or painful experience comes,

the crucial thing is not always

to find the right answers,

but to ask the right questions. . . .

Often it is simply

the right question

at the right time

that propels us into

the journey of awakening.

SUE MONK KIDD

I know how hard your life is right now.

I'm praying that God will encourage you

and transform this difficult time

into a "journey of awakening."

The word *courage* comes from

the Latin word for *heart*—

and courage is born in the heart.

Courageous acts come

from the heart. And a courageous

life is lived from the heart.

So live your life from your heart,

and you will find the courage

you need entwined in your living.

Have confidence in God's mercy,

for when you think

He is a long way from you,

He is often quite near.

THOMAS À KEMPIS

(WHEN YOU ARE

A FRAID)

Courage is the capacity to go ahead in spite of the fear.

SCOTT PECK

I will be there to help you
face your fears. God has already
provided all you need. Let me
help you find courage. It is there
waiting — deep inside you, put
there by the One who loves you —
but your fear is blinding you.

There is so much unknown in our lives; it is only natural
to feel frightened. Like an animal caught in the headlights
of oncoming doom, we stand frozen, staring helplessly,
trying to see the path ahead before we dare to take a step,
and all the while, life rushes at us. . . .
When you find yourself terrified, ask, "What should I do?"
the answer is far more simple than you think.

Your heart is beating with God's love;

open it to others.

He has entrusted you with gifts and talents;

use them for His service.

He goes before you each step of the way;

walk in faith.

Take courage.

Step out into the unknown

with the One who knows all.

to encourage means to:

STRENGTHEN

FORTIFY

INSPIRE

CHEER

NOURISH

NUDGE

REASSURE

You are my hiding place;

you will protect me from trouble

and surround me with

songs of deliverance.

PSALM 32:7

When fear fills your heart,

may you hear God's song of deliverance

and be encouraged.

(WHEN YOU ARE

*O*VERWHELMED)

It is difficulties that show what people are.

EPICURUS

A burden, even a small one,

when carried alone and

in isolation can destroy us,

but a burden when carried

as part of God's burden can

lead us to new life. That is

the great mystery of our faith.

HENRI NOUWEN

May you follow

God's footpath all the way

home to His peace.

You think you cannot make it through one more day.

Struggles, hardships, pain, and difficulty envelop you.

You cry out (to God, to life),

"Please. No more! I can't endure anything else."

Ask yourself: *Can I make it through the next hour?*

If so, put your energy into that, and no more.

If you can't make it through the next hour, can you

endure the next half hour. . .the next fifteen minutes. . .

the next minute?

Then commit yourself to that small space of time

and look no farther ahead. Take hours, minutes, and

moments as they come, one at a time.

Don't run ahead. Do what you can now. . .

and at the end of the day, let it go.

Put all that is left undone in God's hands.

God is at work in ways you cannot see. Trust Him.

Sleep. . .rest. . . Relax in His arms.

Never think that God's delays

are God's denials.

Hold on; hold fast; hold out.

Patience is genius.

COMTE DE BUFFON

Wake each morning
with a sense of hope.
God has amazing things
in store for you.
And He does all things
well.

Resolve to see the world

on the sunny side,

and you have almost

won the battle of life

at the outset.

SIR ROGER L'ESTRANGE

Take your everyday, ordinary life—
your sleeping, eating, going-to-work,
and walking-around life—
and place it before God as an offering.

ROMANS 12:1 THE MESSAGE

It is not what happens that matters,
but how you take it.

HANS SELYE

Every spirit builds itself a house,
and beyond its house a world,
and beyond its world a heaven.
Know then that world exists for you.

RALPH WALDO EMERSON

To be glad of life,

because it gives you the chance

to love and to work and to play

and to look up at the stars. . .

to think. . .every day of Christ;

and to spend as much time as you can,

with body and with spirit,

in God's out-of-doors—

these are little guideposts

on the footpath to peace.

HENRY VAN DYKE

Don't get so busy that you forget to simply *be*.

Sometimes the best way to stop being

overwhelmed by life is to simply step back,

take a day. . .or an hour. . .or a moment,

and notice all that God is doing in your life.

When we take time to notice the simple things in life,

we never lack for encouragement.

We discover we are surrounded by limitless hope

that's just wearing everyday clothes.

ANONYMOUS

(W H E N

Y O U   A R E

*S*ORROWING)

Have courage for the great sorrows of life and patience for the small ones; and when you have laboriously accomplished your daily tasks, go to sleep in peace. God is awake.

VICTOR HUGO

Let him have all your worries and cares,

for he is always thinking about you

and watching everything that concerns you.

1 PETER 5:7 TLB

As a young girl, my daughter often struggled with the experiences that came her way. At bedtime, we always talked about the particular struggles or problems she had faced that day. Our conversations usually led us to the conclusion that she could grow strong in character as she dealt with each day's problems. What looked like problems were really chances for her to grow.

But one day she came home from school obviously frustrated and overwhelmed. When I asked her what was wrong, her answer was loud and immediate:

"I'm tired of these character-building experiences!"
We all have those moments. We're only human—and we do get tired. But as an adult, my daughter is truly strong of character. God used her difficult times to help create the woman she is today. And He will do the same for you and me.

VIOLA RUELKE GOMMER

Character cannot be developed

in ease and quiet.

Only through experience

of trial and suffering

can the soul be strengthened,

vision cleared,

ambition inspired,

and success achieved.

HELEN KELLER

We need time to dream, time to remember,

and time to reach the infinite.

Time to be.

GLADYS TABER

Each of us may be sure that

if God sends us on stony paths

He will provide us with strong shoes,

and He will not send us out on any journey

for which He does not equip us well.

ALEXANDER MACLAREN

I know how much you're hurting right now.

If I could, I'd take the pain away. But I can't.

So instead I'm praying that God will provide

you with "heart-shoes" strong enough

to withstand even the sharpest stones.

The Lord's mercy often rides

to the door of our heart

upon the black horse of affliction.

CHARLES SPURGEON

. . .I have been deprived of peace; I have forgotten

what prosperity is. . . . My soul is downcast within me.

Yet this I call to mind and therefore I have hope:

Because of the Lord's great love we are not consumed,

for his compassions never fail. They are new every morning;

great is your faithfulness. I say to myself,

"The Lord is my portion; therefore I will wait for him."

Lamentations 3:17–18, 20–26

(WHEN LIFE

SEEMS

HOPELESS)

Still round the corner

there may wait,

a new road,

or a secret gate.

J. R. R. Tolkien

How great is the love the Father has lavished on us,

that we should be called children of God!

And that is what we are!

1 JOHN 3:1

Don't let life discourage you;

everyone who got where he is

had to begin where he was.

ROGER L. EVANS

He restores my soul.

PSALM 23:3

Our greatest glory consists not in never falling,

but in rising every time we fall.

OLIVER GOLDSMITH

❧

"Everything is possible

for him who believes."

MARK 9:23

Because we are often spiritually blind,

we fail to see God's hand at work.

God is there, though, present where we least expect Him.

My prayer is that God will surprise you today.

In your daily routine, in the stressful details of ordinary life,

when you least expect it, may grace leap out at you,

encouraging your heart.

Even when you

are discouraged,

hold on to your dreams.

(They have no expiration date.)

May you see
the angels' hands
at work in
your life!

❧

Be encouraged—

for the Giver of Good Things,

the Renewer of Hope,

and the Dispenser

of Wonderful Surprises

is on your side.

He loves you. . .

and He never fails.

When your way seems long and hard,

and you are tempted to give up, remember:

You are not alone.

Jesus is walking at your side.

Trust Him to lead you home

to everylasting peace and joy.

Everything we call a trial, a sorrow, or a duty,

believe me, that an angel's hand is there.

Fra Giovanni

God came to us because God

wanted to join us on the road,

to listen to our story, and to

help us realize that we are not

walking in circles but moving

toward the house of peace and joy.

THOMAS MERTON

When we face

the worst that can happen

in any situation, we grow.

When circumstances

are at their worst,

we can find our best.

ELIZABETH KUBLER-ROSS & DAVID KESSLER

When difficulties and disappointments

come my way, I ask myself two questions:

How can this be used for good?

and

What is the lesson in this for me?

Of course, I always ask a third question as well:

Why me?

But there is really no answer to that question.

So I go back to the first two questions.

They help me accept the situation;

they show me the positive side;

they direct me toward concrete action.

Most of all, they help me to move on.

VIOLA RUELKE GOMMER

God may be invisible,

but He's in touch.

You may not be able to see Him,

but He is in control. . . .

That includes all of life —

past, present, future.

CHARLES SWINDOLL

Even in the winter, even in the midst of the storm,

the sun is still there. Somewhere, up above the clouds,

it still shines and warms and pulls at the life buried

deep inside the brown branches and frozen earth.

The sun is there! Spring will come!

The clouds cannot stay forever.

GLORIA GAITHER

© 2003 by Barbour Publishing, I

ISBN 1-58660-81

Interior images: ©Photonica. Page 4, Valerio Gates; pages 10, 12, 40, 44, Kamil Vong
pages 30-31, Justin Hutchinson; page 38, Patrick McDuno

Book design by Kevin keller; designconcep

Published by Barbour Books, an imprint of Barbour Publishing, In
P.O. Box 719, Uhrichsville, Ohio 44683. www.barbourbooks.c

Printed in Chi
5 4 3